Rave Reviews for
SHINE: *A Simple Philosophy for Success*

"*SHINE: A Simple Philosophy for Success* will warm your heart, lift your spirits and renew your faith in what can happen in your organization when people assume responsibility, expect to win, are willing to be uncomfortable, understand what they want, ask the right questions and focus on what they can control. Paul Huff has written a simple, yet profound book, on the REAL problem with the American workforce."
~ *Craig Daugherty, Vice President of Sales - Mulvanney Homes*

"Don't let the size of this book deceive you. Paul Huff's *SHINE: A Simple Philosophy for Success* might just become the preeminent book in creating the kind of energized and empowered workforce needed to win in business today. Jammed packed with strategies that will improve the performance of every employee in your organization, you'll find yourself wishing you had a ton of "Shines" on your team." ~ *Wray Farlow, Vice President of Sales - Shea Homes*

"Remarkable! In *SHINE: A Simple Philosophy for Success*, Paul Huff has taken seven principles for success exhibited by an amazing shoeshine man, and made them a wonderful guide for improving morale, attitude and customer service in any organization." ~ *Barbara Cheek, Chief Financial Officer - Homeowners Loan Corporation*

"Every year or so, a great book comes along that changes how we look at our business and our lives. *Who Moved My Cheese, Fish* and *Gung Ho* have been recent contributions to this library. After reading Paul Huff's new book, I'm betting you'll agree that *SHINE: A Simple Philosophy for Success* is this year's great book." ~ *Randy Pool, Executive Vice President - New Century Mortgage Corporation*

"The simple principles taught in this book, expressed through the life of an extraordinary shoeshine man – are profound and right on the money. If every employee in America worked with "Shine's" attitude, productivity, profits and customer service would soar. If you're a leader or manager, you should buy every one of your employees this book and have them memorize it." ~ *Brian Gendron, Vice President and General Manager - Hendrick Lexus Automotive*

"Paul Huff has addressed so much in this remarkable book. I have found in *SHINE: A Simple Philosophy for Success* the answers to what ails Corporate America – employee attitudes and morale. A real practical storybook for everyone who wants to learn what it takes to have a fulfilling career and life. A brilliant and simple book. ~ *Doug King, Principle - Straub and King Retirement Planning*

"Almost everyone knows that 'attitude' is the key ingredient to success in business, but nobody knows how to articulate what attitude is, where it comes from and how to present it to an organization like Paul Huff. In his new book *SHINE: A Simple Philosophy for Success*, Paul demonstrates seven attitude principles that will dramatically transform productivity and profits in any company that chooses to implement them. After reading *SHINE*, I am certain that you will not only walk away with some valuable insight into the world of motivation and performance, you will also be committed to a higher standard for yourself and your organization." ~ *Ellen R. Linares, CLU - Northwestern Mutual Financial Network*

SHINE
A Simple Philosophy for Success

Paul Huff

PURE HEART PRESS
MAIN STREET RAG PUBLISHING COMPANY
CHARLOTTE, NORTH CAROLINA

ISBN: 1-930907-85-0

Pure Heart Press/
Main Street Rag Publishing Company
4416 Shea Lane
Charlotte, NC 28227
www.MainStreetRag.com

Dedication

As you read this book, you will discover that the word, "shine" has multiple meanings. First of all, "Shine" is the nickname for the central character in the book. Secondly, you will discover how you can "shine" or stand out from the pack by applying the principles in the book. It is only fitting, then, that I dedicate this book to the light that shines brightest in my life - my wife, best friend, business partner and biggest promoter, Kim Huff. I couldn't do any of this without you sweetheart. I love you.

CONTENTS

Acknowledgments

I am grateful to my friend and mentor, Jim Norman, who believed in this book from day one, and whose insights about everything it seems are always on target. I want to thank Julie Norman for her willingness to take this book on as an editorial project when she really didn't have time to do it. I know you are highly in-demand, Julie, and I feel privileged that you fit me in between all the things you do for Zig. I am grateful to all the people who read the original manuscript and provided invaluable feedback, including Brian Gendron, Gwen Whitley, Randy Pool, Craig Daugherty, Laura Hampton, Robyn Crigger, Ellen Linares, Brad Boughman, and of course, Kim Huff. They all deserve a round of applause. I want to thank my publicist, Patricia Pollack, for not just providing her editorial, layout and PR expertise, but for continuing to exceed my expectations on every project we do together. Finally, I am grateful to the Spirit of the Universe. When I have the sense to pay attention, the path you suggest is ALWAYS the right one.

Foreword

When Paul Huff asked me to write the foreword for *Shine: A Simple Philosophy for Success*, I was pleased for several reasons. First of all, I consider Paul a personal friend. I first met Paul several years ago when he was making his transition from a senior executive in the financial services industry to being a full-time author and speaker. I was immediately struck by a couple of things: Paul is a savvy businessman. Paul genuinely cares about other people. Paul is much more than a motivational speaker; he is a world-class thinker in the psychology of motivation and achievement.

The second reason I am excited about writing this foreword is that Paul's new book has the potential to be the definitive text for helping managers deal with the biggest problem in Corporate America today – whining and complaining. You see, for the past 25 years, I have been a student, not only of the personal and professional development business, but also a student of attitudes among workers in America. Mergers, acquisitions, downsizing, restructuring, outsourcing, and trying to do more with less have all contributed to a different mindset among today's employees. Today's employee is less trusting and more cynical. They blame more and take less responsibility for their own success. Many are finding it difficult to find any real meaning in what they do. Study after study concludes that a very high percentage of the American workforce is dissatisfied. In fact, a recent study conducted by global human resource consultant Towers Perrin reported that workers have a strong emotional connection to work experience, but it's mostly negative.

According to the study, negative emotion about work not only relates to higher turnover rates, but also contributes to the kind of workplace malaise that can materially diminish productivity and performance. In measuring the nature and intensity of employees' emotions about work, the study showed that, on average, more than half of people's current emotion is negative and a third is intensely negative.

Equally disturbing, fully a quarter of the intensely negative employees plan to remain with their current employer — suggesting that the company could have a large segment of disaffected workers simply "hanging on" to their jobs and potentially adversely affecting other employees — and customers — with their negative attitudes.

When you read, *Shine: A Simple Philosophy for*

Success, whether you are a manager or otherwise, you will discover all the key ingredients for winning in today's business climate. And, I'm betting that after you read this book, you'll go out and buy one for all your employees and friends.

Every once in a while, a special speaker comes along who is able to help people blast through barriers that may have been holding them back for years. Paul Huff is one of those special people.

Every once in a while, a special book comes along that touches lives in a way that helps people see their lives and careers in a whole new light. *Shine: A Simple Philosophy for Success* is one of those special books.

Enjoy!

Jim Norman, Norman Services Corporation
Past President, Zig Ziglar Corporation

Introduction

Samuel "Shine" Robinson shines shoes at his own shoeshine stand in the shadow of skyscrapers in the heart of corporate America. I met him several years ago for the first time enroute to a business meeting. My experience with Shine that day left a lasting impression about the power of attitude, expectations and success. His simple philosophy for success is about applying principles that are critical to making our lives and careers what we want them to be.

Businesses and organizations across America suffer because their personnel are consumed by negative thinking and fear that manifests itself in whining and complaining. If you own an enterprise, manage an enterprise, or are employed by an enterprise (this covers about 90% of the U.S. population), this is a subject you should take very seriously. It's challenging to succeed under the best of circumstances but success is made even more difficult by people who habitually look for and then broadcast far and wide all the reasons something is destined to fail. You need a plan to fight and root out whining and complaining because it undermines productivity, accomplishment and success!

Before becoming a professional speaker and author, I enjoyed a 25-year career with one of the largest banks in America. As a Senior Vice President, my most critical objective was to create an environment that would nurture productive attitudes and snuff out whining and complaining wherever it raised its ugly head. I learned early in my career that a bad attitude will consistently undermine and overshadow talent and technical ability. If I have the choice between hiring and working with a skilled person with a bad attitude, or a less trained person with a great attitude, I'll take the person with the great attitude every time. Unfortunately, most businesses don't have the luxury of hiring solely on the basis of attitude. Today's competitive business climate demands that people have skills and experience to be successful. So, what every organization really needs is a lot of people with great attitudes *and* skills.

Shine's simple philosophy for success - let's call it *SHINE* - will help you to nurture an attitude that will lead to positive thinking, productive behavior and higher levels of success. *SHINE* is about winning!

****

Pleasure in the job puts perfection in the work.

~ Aristotle ~

****

SHINE

The day I met Samuel "Shine" Robinson was a crazy day for me. I was on my way to a business meeting and I was concerned about being late. My mind was racing and I was fully involved in thinking about the meeting. Was I ready? Did I have everything I needed? Did I look good? Hmmm. That's when I noticed the dust on my shoes.

I had parked in a gravel parking lot and I had picked up a solid film of dust from toe to heel on both shoes. I thought it was too late to do anything about it, except wipe them off and press on.

Then, out of the corner of my eye, I noticed a one-man shoeshine stand! Even though I was pressed for time, I decided to have the dusty shoe problem taken care of professionally. That's when I met Shine.

As I approached the shine stand, the operator was just finishing with a customer and the chair was immediately available to me. I mounted the stand and took my place in the chair. I thought, "I sure hope this guy works fast...I need to be on my way."

But this shine man was not in a hurry. He was only concerned about giving me the best shoe shine possible.

The slim elderly shine man said, "How you doing, sir? It's a beautiful day, huh? People out and about. Business is good. Un-huh. I've been in this line of work for most of my life. Guess that'd be a lot of years," he chuckled. "Got my own shoeshine stand a few years ago. I like being in business for myself, yes sir. No one to answer to but me and my customers. What line of business did you say you was in?"

I hurriedly told him about my business and got back to worrying about how long the shoeshine might take.

"By the way, the name's Robinson. Samuel Robinson. 'Course most people just call me Shine," he said as he offered me his hand. "Nice to meet you, sir."

Now I was really getting worried. I was thinking, "Shine, yea shine, *that's* what I need. Get with the program, pal," when I suddenly looked down and noticed that Shine was massaging my feet. It felt good. Real good.

I relaxed a bit, decided to read a magazine that was lying on the seat beside me, and just let Shine do his thing.

"Uh, mister," asked Shine.

"Yes," I answered.

"You can read that old magazine anytime, can't you?" he asked with a smile. "I'd rather you watch me work now. I like for people to see what I do. I enjoy shining shoes and I want you to enjoy the experience. Can you see what I'm doing all right? 'Cause you're getting ready to see a big difference in your shoes in just a few minutes."

Then, as I lowered the magazine and started watching him perform magic on my size 14 shoes, he told me about his business.

Samuel Robinson was 12 years old when he started shining shoes. After a time, he got to practice his profession at the airport. He was one of several men working there, but Shine had harbored a dream of someday owning his own shoeshine stand. He wanted to be independent, build a good business, and have the freedom of doing things the way he wanted to do them.

And what Shine wanted to do most of all was give his customers the best shoeshine of their lives. Not just once, but every time he got the opportunity to shine a customer's shoes. Shine *expected* his customers to come back, because he gave them far more than a shoe shine. He gave his customers an *experience!*

As Shine worked on my shoes, it became obvious how much he loved his work. He kept up a constant chatter. He would laugh at his own words as he popped his shine rag and periodically evaluated how my shoes were improving under his professional attention.

When my shoes reached perfection by Shine's standards, he stepped away and smiled. "What do you think?" he asked. I told him my shoes looked fantastic and I really enjoyed my experience. Shine said that was what he always expected to hear from his customers and then he invited me to come back often.

A Simple Philosophy
for Success

My first encounter with Shine Robinson was many years ago but his attitude had a long term affect on me.

I worked in the banking industry for a quarter of a century, eventually rising to the level of Senior Vice President with a significant number of people working for me. I spent most of that time trying to instill Shine's simple philosophy for success in all of my associates.

What is this philosophy? Well, it's pretty simple. *SHINE* is an expectation mindset that good things are going to happen as a result of doing the right things. People who incorporate these principles just do a lot better than people who don't.

Paul Huff

Later in this book I'll go into more detail about all of the principles that support this philosophy, but for now it's enough to say that the most important principle is this: People who believe in themselves and are confident in their ability to achieve their dreams are more successful than people who don't.

The reason is simple: People who believe they will win expect to win! And, I have believed for many years, based on my work with tens of thousands of people, that the expectation of winning is the primary catalyst for consistent success. The expectations we have about our future drive our thinking, our choices and our behavior. Our expectations are the engine of our results. We are going to get what we expect!

People who *SHINE* expect to win. People who do not *SHINE* expect disaster and difficulty. Gloom and negativity dominate their thinking and they frequently become whiners and complainers.

I shared my concern about morale in Corporate America with Shine. He said, "Folks are comfortable talking up here on my stand. They tell me what's on their mind. Most of 'em not too happy with their jobs, I guess. Complaining about this or that. Blaming the company or their boss for their unhappiness. I always remember what my momma used to say. She'd say, 'Samuel, happiness is nothing more than an attitude of mind. It's all about being determined to be happy despite the situation you're in."

Shine thought for another minute, and then said, "I think people ought to find something they love to do. Or start finding a way to love what they're doing now if they want to be happy. 'Course I don't say this to my customers. No sir, I'm just here to give them a great shoeshine. They want to complain and blame. That's their business."

The amount of money that businesses spend trying to teach their employees what Shine has known for years is astronomical. The problem is that people do not share their negative attitudes as openly at work as they do when they are sitting in Shine's shoe shine stand. Whining and complaining can be camouflaged and presented in forms that are not obvious.

****

"High expectations are the key to everything."

~ Sam Walton ~

****

Whining Can Be Deceptive

Traditionally, when we think of whining and complaining the mental image of a pouting two-year-old child comes to mind. That obvious behavior is not tolerated in adults, so people develop more sophisticated forms of whining.

Unfortunately, the end results of both kinds of whining are absolutely the same: *A dramatic reduction in productivity and achievement.* In today's economy, reduced productivity and poor achievement translates into a diminished ability to compete and win!

I'm not a psychologist, but I have raised several children. It's pretty obvious when a two-year-old child is pouting and whining about something. There are essentially three reasons for whining:

1. The child is upset because he/she **did not get** what they want.

2. The child is upset because he/she is afraid they **might not get** what they want.

3. The child is afraid because he/she **expects** something bad to happen to them.

People grow up but they don't always grow out of their childhood fears. Every adult will experience not getting what they want or the fear of not getting what they want and many of those disappointments happen in the workplace. Consider this list of a dozen situations that can lead to whining and complaining.

1. A coveted promotion is not received.

2. An expected raise in salary does not come, or is an amount less than expected.

3. When other people's recommendations are considered superior.

4. When there is public criticism of performance.

5. When lots of people are being "downsized."

6. When formerly internal functions are outsourced.

7. When the boss is cold or abrupt.

8. When leadership communication is inadequate or careless.

9. When suggestions are ignored.

10. When communication is secretive.

11. When truthful information is absent or withheld.

12. When credit due is given to others.

Each of these things happen every day in businesses across our nation and around the world. And, every day people are responding in ways that are counter-productive. It's not that people stick out their lower lip and stomp their feet. No, the whining is much more subtle and that is the problem.

The whining masquerade takes many forms, but they are easily recognized if you understand the symptoms that expose them. The key to identifying this creative form of whining is to remember that people are doing what they are doing because they don't think they are getting what they believe they need or want and they really expect things to happen that will not be good for them. When a person experiences these feelings, they actually believe their well-being is being threatened and the response is to fight or run. In a business environment, the visible behavior will either be defensive or aggressive. Think of the pouting, whining two-year-old either stomping and screaming or sitting in a corner with a protruding lower lip and a big frown on the face. In a business setting, this behavior translates into:

1. Constant negative attitudes about management, customers and co-workers.

2. A company environment filled with rumors and half-truths.

3. People who just don't want to take responsibility for their mistakes.

4. Micro-management of simple tasks and people.

5. Overly rigid interpretations of policy and regulations.

6. The absence of employee suggestions and creativity.

7. Excessive competitiveness between co-workers and leaders.

8. Organizations that resist new ideas.

9. An unwillingness to take risks.

10. Excessive absenteeism.

I'm sure this list could be longer, but these are the most obvious forms of corporate whining. People who *SHINE* in their lives experience the exact opposite of what is listed above. Because they believe in good things, they have expectations of good things and the results they achieve flow from their great expectations.

I've spent over 30 years studying and thinking about the origins of attitude in human beings. It has been a burning question for me and I continue to refine my understanding to this very day.

Shine Robinson's attitude is what captured my attention all those years ago. Not long ago, I asked Shine about attitude.

He said, "Attitude is all about how you feel about yourself. People with a good attitude feel good about themselves and what they're doing. People who don't feel good about themselves, they're the ones doing the complaining. Can you imagine me complaining to my customers? I'd soon be out of business. I don't do that because I feel good about myself and I love what I do. All those folks with a bad attitude ought to try being in business for themselves. Wouldn't last a day. Nobody wants to do business with a person with a bad attitude, I don't care how well you might do the other parts of your job."

Shine's answer confirmed once again what I've concluded, and that is that the origin of attitude is a very simple concept that can become quite complicated when you consider its depth and application to life. Attitude begins with the things we believe.

A Life of Merger and Acquisition

During my banking career, life was an ongoing progression of merger and acquisition. Merger was the bank's primary growth strategy and it was aggressively pursued with focus and determination. No sooner would we survive absorbing one bank than another new acquisition would loom on the horizon. Our work environment was one of constant change. Departments would be combined, split, moved and shuffled on a regular basis. This kind of disruption became our normal operating environment and it went on for years.

As the endless parade of mergers marched through our lives, I noticed a repeatable pattern in people's attitudes. It was almost as if everyone who worked there could be placed into two groups.

Group 1: the Noways: People who were convinced their jobs were in danger and they would soon be on the street. These people would stick to that opinion regardless of the facts.

Group 2 - the Okays: People who always believed things were going to work out well for them in the end, regardless of circumstances.

The Noways feared the future, never seemed to have a good attitude about anything and spent most of their time as if they were emotionally paralyzed. The Okays, who believed everything would eventually work out well for them maintained a good attitude and were productive through all kinds of change, turmoil, and confusion.

The conditions that impacted and influenced both groups were identical. The only difference was how they viewed the future. Okays had such positive expectations about their future that even when some of them lost their jobs through downsizing, they moved on with a smile on their face. They always seemed to be excited about the new opportunities that lay before them and they believed they would prosper, even if they had to endure some temporary difficulties. The Okays believed in themselves and their belief produced great expectations about the future – circumstances seemed to be irrelevant.

The Noways, on the other hand, would remain in a state of gloom long after a merger was concluded, even if they had suffered no loss in pay, position, or authority. They were always waiting for the other shoe to drop and confirm their suspicions about a gloomy future. As they formed mental images of being unemployed, broke and on the street with no visible means of support, these folks eagerly dove into the camouflaged whining and complaining activities I previously discussed. Noways did not seem to believe in themselves and their expectations of the future were quite dismal – regardless of the facts! It was almost as if their primary career objective was to remain as depressed as possible and to pursue every scrap of evidence to support their misery.

The observations I made during those years with the bank confirmed in detail what I now believe to be the biggest single factor in attitude – the expectations that people have about their future drive their attitude. Attitude determines behavior and behavior determines the results people get. Ultimately, the most important issue of productivity and success for a business is attitude.

The foundational issue, however, is to understand where people get their expectations. Why do some people think their future is full of good things and other people believe they are moving downhill on a steep slope to disaster and ruin? Well, I think the answer is quite simple. The Okays, or Group 2 people, the people who have great expectations, all *SHINE*.

A Little *SHINE*
Goes a Long Way

W hen I visited Shine's shoe shine stand for the first time, one thing was perfectly clear: Samuel "Shine" Robinson expected his life to be good and he expected to be the best shoe shine man he could be. He expected good things to happen to him and his future was bright.

When Shine worked at the airport shine stand as an employee, he maintained the dream of starting his own business. He expected it to happen. He had confidence in himself. He believed in his ability and he knew he had the capacity to reach his goals. Shine had a good picture of himself in his mind and could visualize himself operating his own shine stand, giving the best shoe shines in the world and creating a large clientele of repeat customers in the process.

Why did Shine have such positive expectations about his future and eventually accomplish his dreams? Because he was a man who was confident in his ability. He was sure of his capacity for work and excellence. Shine believed in Shine! His belief in himself was the engine for his expectations about the future. Shine knew that he could succeed regardless of circumstances and even though he might experience difficulties and setbacks, he knew his own ability would see him through to better days. *SHINE* is all about having great expectations of the future!

The Belief Machine

The things we believe influence the way we respond to *everything* that happens in our lives. From the day we are born, we begin collecting information based on our experiences. The things we believe emerge from all that we interpret about our experience. Our brain forms the repository for all the information gleaned from the events of our lives and it can hold on to our interpretations of those events for a long, long, time. The brain, as it functions in its role as a repository for life events, becomes something I call The Belief Machine.

We are all very interested in the things that happen to us, which impact our ability to get what we think we want and need. Whenever we have positive experiences that work in our favor, memories of the people, places and things that produced those positive experiences are saved in our Belief Machine. When bad things happen, we likewise record and save the particulars of those events as well.

During the early years of our lives, based on positive and negative experiences we develop all the things we believe to be true, false, right, wrong, good and bad. We decide what we believe is appropriate, inappropriate, acceptable and unacceptable.

Typically, the older we get, the more entrenched our beliefs become and some of our beliefs are so deeply held it seems they are almost impossible to change. For this reason, change is difficult and fearful to embrace.

Real change usually requires us to change things we believe. As a matter of fact, I submit that our ability to change is *always* contingent on being able to change things we believe.

Nobody Gets It Right
All the Time

People get into arguments because they disagree with each other. They disagree because they believe different things to be true concerning whatever it is they are disagreeing about! An argument or disagreement is actually a process wherein opposing parties are trying to change what the other party believes to be the truth. The disagreement ends when one of the parties becomes convinced that the thing they so fervently believed to be true was not true. One of the parties becomes willing to let go of the belief that was fueling the conflict and accept the other party's version of the truth.

I've created a theoretical example of how these kinds of disagreements can be hatched and grow into unpleasant situations. The example centers on a day that is recognized in most work environments - Administrative Professionals Day.

For our example, let's say that Joe's assistant, Patsy has a really big thing about Administrative Professionals Day. Patsy likes to get flowers, but Joe has a serious mental block about Administrative Professionals Day. To Joe, it's just not that big of a deal. However, Patsy has made it very clear to Joe that this is very important to her and she really wants to receive some flowers in recognition and appreciation for her efforts. Patsy says flowers confirm to her that Joe cares about her work and respects her professionally. The flowers make her feel warm, happy and secure in her job. When she does not get flowers she believes it signifies that Joe just doesn't care. The stage is now set for one of those relationship train wrecks.

Two weeks before Administrative Professionals Day, Joe calls a florist and orders a dozen long-stem roses to be delivered to Patsy on the big day. The day before however, the florist spills her iced tea on the stack of handwritten orders and Joe's order for Patsy's roses becomes completely illegible, thus making it impossible to fill.

On Administrative Professionals Day, at the end of the day, Joe is confronted by a disappointed Patsy. It's after 5pm and no flowers have been delivered. Patsy believes that Joe has once again forgotten her.

Joe tries to convince her that he ordered flowers two weeks in advance, and he's dismayed as to why they didn't show up. Joe calls the florist but they don't have any record of his order.

Patsy is hurt and upset. An argument ensues and Joe and Patsy just have a rotten day.

Unfortunately, during the course of their relationship, Joe had forgotten Administrative Professionals Day many times. So many in fact that Patsy expects Joe to forget every year. So, based on her experience with Joe, Patsy really believes that Joe forgot and the story about ordering flowers two weeks in advance is a big lie!

So, there we have it – Patsy believes Joe is lying. Joe stubbornly persists with the claim that he ordered the flowers. This little war will keep raging until Joe can convince Patsy he's telling the truth.

Only when Patsy is able to let go of her sincere belief that Joe is lying will things improve. All of the trouble between Joe and Patsy was rooted in Patsy believing something to be true that was not true.

And, that is the fundamental flaw in our Belief Machine. The Belief Machine is entirely capable of believing things to be true that are not true. Every human being has a lot of stuff filed away in their Belief

Machine they believe is true, but is not. The reason is because we develop our ideas about truth from our experience and our experience is frequently flawed. By flawed, I mean that our experience in any given circumstance may not be typical or normal.

During the course of living our lives, all of us have some bad experiences and some of those experiences are worse than others. Some experiences are just downright horrible. It is the bad or negative events in our lives that cause our Belief Machine to adopt things as truth that may not be true.

For example, a young girl may have experienced abuse from her father. As a result, she may come to believe that all fathers are abusive and that there are no good men in the world. Based on her experience she may believe these things, but they are not really true. Her bad experience is not typical, or normal, but it has created a strong belief in a concept about men and fathers that is abnormal.

It is a huge concept that our beliefs drive our expectations and our expectations create the results we experience in our lives. If we have formed many of our beliefs from a lot of negative experiences, we are going to have negative expectations. When we have negative expectations, can you guess what we are going to get? Right. Negative results.

****

"The squeaking wheel doesn't always get the grease. Sometimes it gets replaced."

~ Source Unknown ~

****

NO, NO, NO!

In the case of children growing up, most of their experience is restrictive. Kids hear the "no" word a lot! While it's necessary to discipline children, many parents miss the mark on balancing their "no" language with an equal amount of encouragement and positive affirmation.

A lot of children have grown up in America during the past 50 years or so with beliefs that won't allow them to have positive expectations about their future. They believe they aren't *smart* enough. They believe they aren't *good* enough. They believe that *trying hard* won't work. They believe all kinds of things that smother any positive expectations and hope they may have for their lives.

Samuel "Shine" Robinson was born in the inner city. His father died before Shine ever got to know him. Most people would agree that Shine's early childhood was challenging.

A loving but determined mother raised Shine and his ten brothers and sisters. "We never had many of the material things other kids had," Shine said, "But we were never short on love. Lots of times it was what you might call tough love, you know, but momma made sure we had what we needed and she taught us responsibility."

As an African American growing up in the 1930s and '40s, Shine surely had bad experiences.

When asked how discrimination affected him, Shine said, "Everybody has to overcome things in their life. I've had to overcome a bunch of things, but I'll tell you what. Instead of making me angry and bitter, it made me realize that I had a choice every time about how I was going to react to the situation. I can't tell other people what to do or how to act. That's on them. But how I choose to react, that's all on me."

His mother had a very positive influence and taught him that he could have a dream and that he could achieve that dream. She taught Shine the principles of helping others. She taught him courage and the disciplines of patience and hard work that allowed him to persevere until the day he could start his own business. She taught him to look at life and life's experience in a positive light. She taught him that he could choose the way he would interpret the events of this life and that the choices he made would shape his success or failure.

And that, I think, is the lesson for all to see: our Belief Machine can be influenced by the way we *choose* to interpret and view the events of our lives.

Our Belief Machine is not really in control of us. We all have the ability to shape the input that goes into our Belief Machine and no matter how bad or negative the input of our past has been, we can begin to shape new input today and acquire a vision to see life as an amazing possibility, rather than a curse. We can literally determine the things we believe by making decisions that will create changes in the way we respond to our experience.

When we can recognize the futility and the damage we do to ourselves and to our success by dwelling on past injury and insult, it puts us in a position to become willing to do some things differently. But after a lifetime of making bad choices in response to the negative events in our life, it may take some time to change things and develop new ways to respond. Responding to negative events in a less than positive way is human nature and the intuitive way we tend to respond to negative things.

However, life is short and the truth is that we can _choose_ to respond differently to negative events, so that we can change our beliefs and create positive expectations about the future. And, as we have seen – positive expectations just give us better results in everything we do.

Back to Whining and Complaining

Now that we understand how our Belief Machine works and how it soaks up the input we provide it from our experience, we can see how our expectations about the future are formed. When we consider all of the camouflaged whining and complaining that goes on in businesses and organizations that is negatively impacting the collective ability to win, we are faced with a question. How does the Belief Machine play into all of this whining and complaining?

Simple. It means that the people who are whining and complaining are making choices that allow their Belief Machines to create negative beliefs that fuel bad attitudes and produce a lot of negative expectations.

The prescription for overcoming whining and complaining (and all of the camouflaged versions) is to become willing to make different choices in the way we respond to the events of our lives.

Easier said than done? Honestly...yes. However, it is well worth the effort. When we really understand and come to believe that learning how to make positive choices can revolutionize our attitudes and produce wonderful expectations for living, it's worth giving up the misery we inflict on ourselves.

SHINE captures the concept of having the willingness to look at life with a new perspective that changes the focus from negative response to positive expectation. We must take control of our Belief Machine by controlling the input we allow to reach it. We must be like Shine. We have to have faith in our ability to overcome any negative event and see the opportunity and good that always comes from overcoming.

Experience is a great teacher, but we can decide what kind of students we will be, and how we interpret that experience. Shine recognizes there are higher paying jobs with more prestige than his chosen career, but he also knows that loving what you do is a key ingredient to success and happiness. One day Shine heard voices behind him. Two young men were trading barbs as they rushed by his stand. "At least we're not shining shoes for a living," one laughed to the other. "That's right," the other fellow agreed. "Things aren't that bad yet."

Shine noticed the young men as they walked past his stand and took seats at a nearby outdoor café. Shine walked over to them after he'd finished up with his customer.

"How you young fellows doing? Name's Shine Robinson. Don't mean to interrupt your lunch but if you gentlemen ever need a shoeshine, I give the best one in town. My stand's right over there," he pointed. "I'd be happy to serve you anytime."

Shine said the young men squirmed a bit in their seats as he continued to smile down at them. "You know, I guess a lot of folks would be ashamed to shine shoes for a living, but not me. I love it. No sir, I ain't ashamed of it. No way! By the way, you fellows have a nice day, okay?"

Once again, Shine provided a real life story perfectly suited to show how a person with the right perspective can take a negative, even potentially hurtful, event and seize the opportunity to turn it into a positive learning experience for the very people who might have harmed him.

****

"We advance on our journey only when we face our goal, when we are confident and believe we are going to win out."

~ Orison Swett Marden ~

****

Seven Qualities of *SHINE*

I've talked about the subtlety of whining and complaining and described various ways it is camouflaged. I've also alluded to the fact that there are specific characteristics and principles that constitute Shine's philosophy for success. This final section deals with the principles and characteristics of that philosophy and also explains how to acquire them.

Once people acquire these characteristics, it is impossible for them to demonstrate behaviors that remotely resemble whining and complaining. This is important because whining and complaining contributes to losing. *SHINE* is about winning!

Let's take a quick look at each of these qualities and see how they helped Shine achieve his dreams and give us a great example of what it takes to win and succeed.

You can *TEST YOUR SHINE* by answering the questions that follow the description of each quality.

Quality 1
Shine Assumes Responsibility

There is an epidemic in America causing people to think they can avoid responsibility for their own actions. I saw an advertisement recently for a weight loss pill in which the announcer assured potential customers that it "is not your fault you are overweight." I don't want to disparage people who struggle with their weight but the last time I heard, eating was a voluntary activity.

It seems that more and more people do not believe they are responsible for anything that is considered negative or improper. Addicted people are victims of disease. People in prison are victims of society and bad parenting. Tobacco companies are now legally liable for the choices of millions of people, who smoke cigarettes despite warnings about the dangers of smoking. Lots of people believe they are not responsible for the bad things that happen to them resulting from their own actions and behavior.

Shine took responsibility for himself. When he worked at the airport for others, he did not consider himself a victim deprived of opportunity. Instead, he saw potential for success and accepted responsibility for doing what he had to do to move on and move up.

Accepting responsibility requires that we look to ourselves for our own solutions and take responsibility for wherever we are and what has happened to us. Don't misunderstand. I know that bad things sometimes happen to good people. The point is that people who know how to accept responsibility have the ability to overcome their difficulty and move on to better times. They do so without playing the blame game. Instead, their focus is on what THEY need to do to change and improve their situation.

TEST YOUR SHINE: Which of the following statements best describes how well you accept responsibility? Circle the number that best represents you:

1. I always blame others for my circumstances. It's certainly not my fault.

2. I frequently find myself blaming others for my circumstance.

3. I sometimes find myself blaming others for my circumstance.

4. I mostly assume responsibility for my decisions, actions, priorities and results.

5. I always assume total responsibility for my decisions, actions, priorities and results.

Quality 2
Shine Expects to Win

Winning to Shine meant having his own shoeshine stand. From the day he conceived that vision, it became a realistic expectation for Shine. There was no doubt in his mind that it would happen.

It is amazing how many people really expect to lose! It is not so amazing to me that those same people usually do lose. They never seem to get what they hope for. Something always seems to happen that causes them to give up. When the going gets tough, they abandon their dream.

Shine had challenges he had to overcome to realize his dream. And I'm certain that when Shine first opened his business he went through the long process of building that business. What carried him through the tough times was his expectation of winning. If we expect to win, we will.

TEST YOUR SHINE: Which of the following statements best describes your expectations? Circle the number that best represents you.

1. I always think the worst. I tend to "disaster fantasize" when a new situation presents itself.

2. I sometimes have a feeling of dread when a new situation presents itself.

3. I usually take a "wait and see" approach to a given situation.

4. I frequently expect things to work out favorably for me, depending on the situation.

5. I always expect things to work out favorably for me, no matter what the situation.

****

"*The lust for comfort, that stealthy thing that enters the house a guest and then becomes a host, and then a master.*"

~ Kahlil Gibran ~

****

Quality 3
Shine Is Willing to Be
Uncomfortable

Sometimes, as we go through life things happen to us that make us uncomfortable. This is true when it comes to confronting obstacles that must be overcome to reach our dreams.

I believe our "comfort zone" is nothing more than a refuge for doing nothing of significance. We all have a comfort zone. The comfort zone is comfortable because there is nothing in it that challenges us or requires us to do something we don't want to do or that we are unfamiliar with. In other words, we don't have to change and that is why the comfort zone feels good. We don't have to stretch. We don't have to challenge our preconceived notions about anything. We can just keep on doing what we have been doing. Unfortunately, it also means we will keep getting the same results.

Winning requires abandoning our comfort zone on a regular basis. Change requires abandoning our comfort zone. If we are unwilling to do things that make us uncomfortable we will not achieve our full potential.

Paul Huff

Comfort zones are also occupied by people who love to do a lot of whining and complaining. What they are really complaining about are things that have the potential to make them uncomfortable! If you go back to the first part of this book and review the symptoms of whining and complaining, it becomes clear that the unwillingness to be uncomfortable is a big support factor for the symptoms.

Shine is willing to be uncomfortable. He could have probably shined shoes at the airport his entire life, made a decent living and been comfortable in that role. It was probably uncomfortable for Shine to quit that job and strike out on his own, to find and negotiate a location for his business, and to set up a shine stand on the street and start over, soliciting business from strangers. Shine is willing to be uncomfortable to get what he wants and expects.

When people learn to be uncomfortable their lives change and the results they experience also change. The new results will help them achieve more and experience greater success.

TEST YOUR SHINE: Which of the following statements best describes how you handle being uncomfortable? Circle the number that best represents you.

1. Why be uncomfortable when you don't have to be? Besides, I'm pretty content and don't really want that much anyway.

2. I frequently find myself moving back into my comfort zone even when I know it's keeping me from accomplishing some of my goals.

3. I sometimes find myself staying in my comfort zone even when I know that means settling for less than I really want.

4. I am willing to be uncomfortable for awhile because I know that discomfort eventually leads to growth.

5. My feeling is that greatness does not come from comfort. I'm striving for greatness in my life so I'm willing to be uncomfortable along the way.

Quality 4
Shine Knows What He Wants

Shine had a clear vision of his dream. He could see himself working at his own stand years before it actually became a reality. He was able to imagine how he would feel operating his own business. He could sense the self-esteem it would give him and he knew being self-employed would be something he could be satisfied with for a long, long time.

He's been shining shoes for more than 60 years now and still says, "I hope the good Lord lets me do this until the day He takes me away. The fact is there's nothing I'd rather be doing. I get up every morning about 3:00, fix me a cup of coffee and start thinking about shining people's shoes. Yes sir, I'm on the job right here at this stand by 5:30 five days a week. You know why? 'Cause a lot of my customers get to work early, too. I wouldn't want them to miss out on getting a great shoeshine."

Shine knows what he wants.

Knowing what we want is a big part of our expectations. Knowing what we want has a specific quality to it. It goes beyond just having an attitude that good things are going to happen. Knowing what we want involves coupling specific definition and description to the things we dare to imagine.

For Shine, knowing what he wanted involved a shine stand that was a certain size and configuration. He knew how he wanted it built and designed to give him the best possible setup to provide the greatest shoe shine.

Knowing what we want goes beyond just wanting **A** shine stand. It involves wanting **THE** shine stand. It involves being able to see it and touch it with our minds. It is only when we can take the things we want to that level that we have the ability to do what needs to be done to get the things we want.

TEST YOUR SHINE: Which of the following statements best describes how well you know what you want? Circle the number that best represents you.

1. I think the whole idea of goal setting is worthless. It just leads to disappointment and frustration.

2. I don't know what I want. I'm more clear on what I don't want.

3. I have a vague idea about what I want to accomplish over the next 12 months.

4. I know what I want but I haven't written it down.

5. I have clearly defined and written down goals for what I want to achieve over the next 12 months.

Quality 5
Shine Asks the Right Questions

To refresh your memory, here are the things Shine Robinson asked me:

- *What line of business did you say you was in?*
- *You can read that old magazine anytime, can't you?*
- *What do you think?*

Three little questions turned me from being a person in a hurry to a person willing to enjoy an experience and become a life-long fan of Shine's wonderful shoe shines. Without those three questions I would have continued reading my magazine, paid Shine and left. I would not know the story of Shine and you would not be reading this book.

When Shine asked me what line of work I was in, he got me thinking about me. I felt like Shine was interested in me as a person. We all like to talk about what we do and Shine invited me to do that. That question opened me up and made me really begin to notice Samuel "Shine" Robinson, the man.

When Shine asked me if I could read that old magazine anytime, it really got my attention. It made me think about why Shine would ask such a question. At that point he had my full attention focused on what he said next. *"I'd rather you watch me work now. I like for people to see what I do. I enjoy shining shoes and I want you to enjoy the experience."*

Now Shine had me exactly where he wanted me! I was riveted to watching him work and my shoe shine had taken on a new importance. I had been transformed from a guy running late to a guy suddenly aware that a life changing experience was underway.

The third question Shine asked, "What do you think?" came when he had finished his work. It was a question that would provide the payoff for the reason Shine started his business. He wanted to make a difference in my life...and he did.

I've been talking about Shine for years in my presentations and seminars. Not only did Shine Robinson change my life, Shine Robinson, through me, has also made a difference in the lives of many thousands of others. All of this happened because Shine asked me the right three questions.

I recently turned the tables on Shine when I asked him a question of my own. I asked him to tell me what makes Shine tick.

"Well, I'd be the best judge of what makes Shine tick because I've been living with the man for more than 80 years now," he laughed.

And then Shine got introspective. "I've got a strong desire inside me to be the best at what I do. My momma gave that to me, I reckon, plus I just love shining shoes and I love making people happy. I know folks can go to a lot of places to get their shoes shined in this town. They don't have to come to my stand. But, if you want to beat the competition, you've got to be better than them. You've got to give your customers a reason to come to you. I expect the reason most people come here is because they believe I give 'em the best shoeshine in town. Maybe not the quickest, 'cause I like to take my time and do things right, you know, but definitely the best. And I'm betting when they leave my stand for the first time, it won't be the last time. Makes me feel good knowing I've done them a great job. Makes that motivation in me even stronger."

Ask questions.   You're almost guaranteed a learning opportunity!

TEST YOUR SHINE: Which of the following statements best describes how you ask questions? Circle the number that best represents you.

1. My questions almost always help me to see the glass as half-empty.

2. My questions sometimes lead me to see roadblocks and obstacles.

3. I really don't know what kind of questions I ask.

4. I sometimes ask questions that open up opportunities and possibilities.

5. I always seem to ask questions that open up opportunities and possibilities.

Quality 6
Shine Focuses on What He Can Control

Shine Robinson did not spend a lot of time worrying about the rising price of shoe polish. Shine Robinson didn't invest his energy considering the problem of suburban sprawl and how that might eventually cut down on the foot traffic in the city where he works. Shine Robinson focused on the things he could do something about.

I understand there is a prayer said by people in recovery from various kinds of addiction that says: *"God, grant me the serenity to accept the things I cannot change, the courage to change the things I can – and the wisdom to know the difference."* We don't have to be suffering from an addiction to put this wonderful concept into practice as a way of life.

It is amazing how worrying about things we can't possibly control takes up so much of our time and energy. Remember the whiners and complainers? Well, that's what they are doing. They are whining and complaining largely about things they can do very little about and it poisons their attitude about the things they CAN do to change things.

Paul Huff

Shine Robinson accepts reality and focuses on the things he can change by his own efforts. He *can* do something about convincing people passing by to stop for a shine. He *can* be sure of his ability to prepare each of his customers for the shine of their life. Shine, by his efforts *can* be what he wants to be: The #1 shoe shine business in his hometown!

Shine is just dealing with what he can control, which is to give his customers the best shoe shine possible. This simple principle is a powerful concept that has the potential of revolutionizing our lives and the results we achieve.

TEST YOUR SHINE: Which of the following statements best describes your focus? Circle the number that best represents you.

1. I frequently worry about things over which I have no control.
2. I sometimes worry about things over which I have no control.
3. I don't think about what I can control and what I can't.
4. I focus on what I can control most of the time.
5. I always focus on what I can control.

Quality 7
Shine Defines His Work in Terms of How to Make a Difference

Shine Robinson told a lot about his real purpose in life when he said, "I'd rather you watch me work now. I like for people to see what I do. I enjoy shining shoes and I want you to enjoy the experience." He wanted people to arrive in one condition and leave in another. I arrived as a hurried business person, almost late for a meeting, who needed to slow down a bit. Shine transformed me into a person watching a great entrepreneur at work who truly loved what he did. I was different when I climbed down from that shoe shine stand and the difference went beyond just having a clean, shiny pair of shoes on my feet.

Shine Robinson inspired me! I believe we make a difference in the lives of others when we inspire them and I believe that we all have the opportunity each day to inspire others. The last time I visited with Shine it became very apparent just how many people he has inspired, or at least befriended.

He continued to work as we talked and at least 20 people passed his stand and gave him a shout or a hearty wave. Several called out, "How're you doing,

Mr. Robinson?" "Good to see you, Shine." "What's happening, Shine?" "Shine, I'll be by to see you in a few days."

One of the gentlemen he was working on overheard my conversation with Shine and said, "My name is Joe Copeland. I've been coming to see Shine for over 20 years. He's not only the best shine man in this town; he is one of the best people I know. The man is honest and he takes enormous pride in what he does. He cares about people. You can see it and you can feel it. Use my name in your book if you want to, but there are lots of people who would tell you the same thing if you ask them. Shine is a special man. No question about it. That's why I keep coming back. That's why a lot of people keep coming back."

I hope I can be such an inspiration to others that one day someone will voluntarily offer similar words of affirmation about me. The truth is we can inspire others in our businesses and in our communities and in our homes. Shine sees every pair of shoes as an opportunity to make a difference. We should see the same kind of opportunity in our own professions and businesses. When we can see our products and services in that perspective, we can accomplish anything we expect and want. And that, in the final analysis, is the magic of Shine's simple philosophy for success.

Paul Huff

TEST YOUR SHINE: Which of the following statements best describes how you define your work? Circle the number that best describes you.

1. I believe the concept is hokey. I've got a "job" to do and I just do it.
2. I have never thought about my job within that context.
3. I sometimes see my job in terms of how I'm making a difference in the lives of others.
4. I frequently view my job in terms of how I'm making a difference in the lives of others.
5. I always view my job in terms of how I'm making a difference in the lives of others.

Your *SHINE* Quality Score

Go back and add up your scores for each of the seven qualities listed. For example, if you circled #3 for the first quality, you would assign a value of 3. If you circled #4 for the second quality, that would equate to a numeric value of 4, and so forth. You should end up with seven scores. The maximum score is 35 (7 qualities X 5), and the lowest score is 7 (7 qualities X 1). If you scored between:

29 - 35 – Congratulations, you already *SHINE* and are no doubt a peak-performing individual. You take responsibility for your success; you have a hopeful and optimistic approach to life; you realize that greatness does not come from comfort; you know precisely what you want; you ask questions that enable you to see opportunities and possibilities; you don't sweat the small stuff; and you have found a way to define your job in terms of how you are making a difference in people's lives.

22 - 28 – You are fast approaching the elite of performers. You usually take responsibility for where you are and what has happened to you; you expect to win more often than lose; you are often willing to explore outside your comfort zone; you think you know what you want; you are not afraid to ask questions; you make an effort to concentrate on the things that matter most and the way you can make a difference in the world around you.

15 - 21 – You are standing still instead of moving in a positive direction. You get the job done, but in an uninspired way; you sometimes blame others and feel that you have little control over your circumstances; you tend to do things the way you've always done them and react to change rather than taking positive action towards making change; you don't think much about goals or what is within your control; and although sometimes you feel that you are making a difference, most of the time you're just trying to get through another day.

7 - 14 – Your behavior is counter-productive. You are making choices that fuel a bad attitude and produce a lot of negative expectations; you don't think you are getting what you believe you need or want and so you expect bad things to happen to you;

you frequently blame others for these bad things and dread new situations where you expect more bad things to happen; you definitely know what you don't want and worry a lot about those things; your fear keeps you trapped within a small space where you feel safe from disappointment and frustration but does not allow you to succeed.

****

"Life... It tends to respond to our outlook, to shape itself to meet our expectations."

~ Richard M. DeVos ~

****

Acquiring *SHINE*

Don't you think the characteristics of Shine's philosophy for success are qualities that you and the people you work with should seek to acquire? What a powerful team of people such conditions would produce.

You might say that such an idea is impossible. I would say that such an idea is **not** impossible. I know it can be done, but it requires having a plan, a workable concept, to make it happen.

Furthermore, I believe the reward potential is so huge, that whatever effort is required is worth the effort. A company or organization full of Shine Robinsons is an awesome force!

There are four specific things people must do to get on the path to change and allow them to *SHINE*.

Paul Huff

It is a process that will create voluntary change in the attitudes and behavior of people and voluntary change is the only kind of change that lasts. Let's briefly examine each of them.

Four Phases for Creating Voluntary Change

Phase 1: Identify the Issue

If people don't understand the issues there is no foundational reason to support personal change. Frankly, a lot of people suffer from a condition of unconscious incompetence.   That just means they 'don't know they don't know.'

If, for example, someone puts a strange machine in front of you and there is no explanation about how it works or what it does – you won't have much use for the machine. It will have no value and will actually be a nuisance because it is taking up space on your desk you could use for something else.

If that machine was a computer you would be ignoring something that has the power to change your life. However, for the computer to reach its potential as a tool for you there must be an understanding of what it does and how it works.   You need to understand how a computer can help you schedule your day, communicate with the world, manage your accounts – you get the picture?   There must be a personal benefit associated with the machine's function to peak your interest.

There also needs to be an understanding of the price being paid for not using the computer. It takes you longer to write letters and memos. You are denied access to an information source that is changing the world. If you don't understand the function and value of a computer you are at a severe career disadvantage. If you happen to own a business you are at a competitive disadvantage.

So, change begins with identifying the issue at hand. It involves overcoming the condition of not knowing and moving forward to the next logical phase of awareness: Knowing that you don't know! People need to be educated on the reality of whining and complaining and the power they can realize when they begin to *SHINE*. Leadership must help them break through to this level of awareness. If this isn't done, they will just continue on in their condition of "not knowing."

Phase 2: Decide It Must Be Done

If people do not voluntarily accept that something MUST be done, nothing will be done! They arrive at this place when they know they don't know something.

Using the computer analogy, they recognize the damage they have unknowingly suffered by not understanding the value of the computer. The sense of loss and need they experience at this revelation is so compelling that they whole-heartedly accept the fact that they must learn how to use the computer.

When people reach this point they will develop a case of what we call 'computer fear'. They will fear that the machine might be smarter than they are and far too difficult to learn how to use.

However, even though they are fearful they recognize there is no choice left for them and they must take on this dreaded task. They must make a decision that it has to be done if they want to succeed and be as successful as possible.

Phase 3: Take Responsibility for Doing It

If people are unwilling to take complete responsibility for change, change will never be voluntary. Once we learn the value and function of the computer and become convinced of our need to learn how to use it, we must accept that it is our responsibility to make it happen. I will have to invest the time in reading, attending classes and practicing long hours to master the machine. My employer might offer all of the materials and classes I need to become competent, but I am the one who has to put forth the effort.

The challenge presented by change always confronts the willingness people have to take full responsibility for making the change. People instinctively seek ways to soften the blow of responsibility for something that might be unpleasant or difficult to achieve. There must be an acceptance that there are resources to help me change, but I must pick up those tools and use them. Nobody can do it for me. Leadership has to encourage people to accept the reality of this truth.

Phase 4: Believe That It Is Possible

When we learn what the computer is and what it can do; when we become convinced we must learn how to use it; and when we accept the fact that we are responsible for learning how to use it, one step remains. We have to believe it is *possible* to learn how to use it. It's not enough to believe that other people can do it. I have to believe that I can do it! It is at the point that I believe that I will begin to actually do it! Belief allows us to *SHINE.*

****

"Remind yourself regularly that you are better than you think you are. Successful people are not superhuman. Success does not require a super-intellect. Nor is there anything mystical about success. And success isn't based on luck. Successful people are just ordinary folks who have developed a belief in themselves and what they do. Never - yes, never - sell yourself short."

~ David J. Schwartz ~

****

The End is the Beginning

I hope you have been persuaded to appreciate the principles of *SHINE: A Simple Philosophy for Success*. More importantly, I hope that you are motivated to help yourself and others move through the four phases of acceptance that will empower you to change your business or organization. Our expectations hold the key to success or failure and I want you to not only win, but to experience a better way of living and working on a daily basis.

Spread the Word and Help Others to *SHINE*

SHINE: A Simple Philosophy for Success is available at special quantity discounts for bulk purchases for sales promotions, premiums, fund-raising, or educational use. For more information, please contact:

Paul Huff International
3020 W. Arrowood Road
Charlotte, NC 28273
704-944-6070